THE THIRD BOOK OF CURRIES

Also written by Harvey Day
and published by Nicholas Kaye

CURRIES OF INDIA

THE SECOND BOOK OF CURRIES

Acknowledgments

I should like to thank all those who have assisted me in collecting material for this book. Their names are given at the end of the recipes they have so kindly supplied.

H. D.

THE THIRD BOOK OF CURRIES

by

HARVEY DAY

Drawings by B. Gerry

NICHOLAS KAYE

LONDON

First published by
NICHOLAS KAYE LIMITED
194–200 Bishopsgate, London, E.C.2
1960

Printed in England by
ADLARD AND SON LIMITED
London and Dorking

Contents

Chapter		Page
1	'A LITTLE OF WOT YER FANCY'	6
2	MISCELLANEOUS HINTS	10
3	DISHES OF BURMA	12
4	DISHES OF CEYLON	19
5	DISHES OF INDIA AND PAKISTAN	31
6	DISHES OF INDONESIA AND THAILAND	35
7	DISHES OF IRAN AND IRAQ	41
8	DISHES OF MALAYA	47
9	DISHES OF TURKEY	54
	ADDRESSES OF CURRY-SPICE SUPPLIERS	62
	INDEX	63

CHAPTER ONE

'A Little of Wot Yer Fancy'

'How a poor woman makes palatable Mince Pyes of stinking Meat.'
None of the recipes in this book deals with the problem. They
have no need to. But in the eighteenth century, before the advent
of refrigeration, meat often went bad, especially in the homes of the
poor who eked out their supplies over weeks; and in his delightful
little book, *Meet Mr Ellis*, Vicars Bell gives extracts, supplemented
by comments, of life in Little Gaddesden, Herts, two centuries ago.

According to Mr Ellis, a prosperous farmer, 'This is a poor
industrious Woman that rents a little Tenement by me of Twenty
Shillings a Year, who for the Sake of her Poverty is Every Week
relieved, with many others, by the most noble Lord of Gaddesden
Manour; who killing a Bullock almost every week for his large
Family, he has the Offald meat dressed, and is so good as to have
it given to the poorest People in the Neighbourhood. But as it
sometimes happes, through the Negligence of careless Servants, that
this charitable meat is apt to stink in hot Weather, for want of its due
cleaning, boiling, and laying in a cool Place. However, the Poor
are very glad of this Dole, as it does their Families considerable
Service.

'And to recover such tainted Meat, this Woman, after boiling and
cleansing it well, chops and minces it very small, and when mixed

6

with some Pepper, Salt, chop'd Sage, Thyme, and Onion, she bakes it: This for a savoury Pye. At another Time she makes a sweet Pye of this flesh, by mixing a few Currants and Plumbs with it. But in either Form the Taint is so lessened that it is hardly to be perceived.'

People in the Far East, however, were never forced to eat tainted food, as tribes in more temperate climates were, for the spices in which they prepared meat, fish and vegetables preserved such comestibles for days, if not weeks, and where mustard oil was used, for months!

Incidentally, according to C. C. Furnas, Associate Professor of Chemical Engineering, Yale University, and S. M. Furnas, formerly Instructor in Nutrition, University of Minnesota, putrefying food is not necessarily harmful and, indeed, many highly civilized peoples like certain dishes rather 'high'. 'The organisms,' say these gentlemen, 'which cause it [putrefaction] are for the most part not harmful to man and the eating of rotten meat is a relatively safe practice provided there has been no contamination *of man's own making*. Many primitive peoples in small communities thrive on it.'

Apparently it's only the uncultured who, knowing nothing about gastronomy, like their food fresh. The gourmet rarely touches a medlar till it is soft and half rotten. To him jugged hare is a delicacy, and in the 'best' clubs and restaurants grouse is hung till infested with maggots.

In his fascinating autobiography, *A Pinch of Pound Notes*, John Dingle, a famous chef, describes how, when he was at the Junior Constitutional Club, one of his chores was to take down and salvage grouse past the peak of their 'prime'.

One evening two portions of cold grouse were ordered: 'A toast *canapé* was made with a slice of toast loaded with *pâté de foie gras* paste prepared from the hearts and livers of the birds. On this were mounted the half bird, small cornets of ham filled with aspic jelly and gherkins. Beetroot salad with bouquets of cress comprised the garnish, with a few game chips.'

Later, a waiter descended to the kitchen and remarked, 'I've never served grouse risotto cold before'.

'What do you mean?' asked Dingle.

'That's what it was, wasn't it?'

'No; it was simply cold, roast grouse.'

'Well,' retorted the waiter, 'I carved them at table; I served the breast and half a *canapé* with salad to each guest, and I could have sworn the carcass was stuffed with risotto.'

Dingle jumped to his feet and rummaged in the waste bin till he found the carcasses, and sure enough they were packed tight with what appeared to be risotto but, in fact, was roast maggots! To his relief, when they had eaten, the diners sent a message down to the chef to say they had seldom tasted grouse more delicious!

People who know nothing about cheeses reel away from Camembert, Roquefort and Stilton because the plebeian proboscis is not equipped to differentiate between the sordid and the sublime.

Delectable as provender that is 'high' or 'ripe' may be, however, there is no need for those who eat curry to sample it—and curry dishes can be even more mouth-watering. Their first appeal is to the nose so that, unlike the dishes already mentioned, one does not have to steel oneself before tasting.

Curry spices were never meant to camouflage tainted flesh or vegetables, but to preserve their freshness in climates where food deteriorates rapidly.

Little work has so far been done on spices and their dietetic value has been ignored. Those who know nothing about them write them off as irritants; but Professor A. G. Winter of Cologne University has done some research on mustard oils, horse-radish and other spices and has discovered that they kill harmful bacteria in the intestines; and when pigs and chickens kept on a diet short of proteins had these spices added to their food they improved in health.

Do they contain some principle which we are not as yet aware of? Dr Barbara Moore proved recently by taking three long walks of 110, 373 and 1000 miles respectively, in rain, sleet and snow, that one can maintain both health and vigour without the traditional bread and meat, for her sole sustenance was honey and water, an egg, carrots, lettuce and tomatoes! Moreover, many in the East live on what we would term a starvation diet, but they don't die; what is more, they keep their health and agility. Is it because of the mustard oil and spices they eat?

Mustard oil contains a little vitamin B12 which is known to prevent anaemia, and when this is rubbed on Indian children, some of the vitamin is absorbed through the skin. Their food, when cooked in mustard oil, must also provide the vitamin.

Almost all curries are eaten to the accompaniment of pickles made with mustard oil, chillies and fresh vegetables or fruit. Often only the oil is heated, and the fruit is raw, thus retaining its vitamin C.

Research on a wide scale should be done on food spices and their contribution to good health should be broadcast. The suggestion that they irritate the membranes of the stomach and intestines and lead to an early grave is sheer rubbish. Millions who eat and enjoy curries that would skin your tongue and palate live to a ripe old age.

Curries are not only eaten in India and Pakistan but in every

8

country where spices are cheap and plentiful. Obviously, they were provided by Nature for man's use and enjoyment, and herbs and spices such as aloe, anise, dill, balm, bay, hyssop, marjoram, cinnamon, coriander, cummin, caper, gall, onion, garlic, leek, mint, mustard, rue, and saffron have Biblical sanction.

In this little book we give you recipes from countries as far west as Turkey and Persia, and as far east as Malaya and Indonesia, embracing more than a quarter of the world's population. They have eaten spiced foods and traded in spices for more than 4000 years, and where there exists a variety of spiced foods and no over-indulgence men live as long as in any other part of the world: sound testimony that such foods are good for you.

There are few surer guides to health than the eye, nose, palate and digestion. When all four are in agreement, then only is that dear old philosopher and physician, Marie Lloyd, vindicated—for did she not trill nightly in music-halls throughout Britain, in terms that even the most unsophisticated could understand, 'A little of wot yer fancy does yer good!'

CHAPTER TWO

Miscellaneous Hints

A Word About Fats

GHEE is clarified butter; that is, butter treated with steam to remove impurities. It tastes different from butter, and once used for cooking will always be preferred.

When mustard oil is used, it must always be heated till a wisp of blue smoke rises from its surface before putting ingredients into it. It is extremely digestible, like olive oil; but make sure you have the grocer's, not the chemist's brand!

For the best results, use ghee, butter, mustard oil or olive oil; but lard, dripping, sessamum, peanut, coconut or soya-bean oil are all permissible. If you find the quantities given make the food too rich, experiment with less.

Curry Ingredients

SPICES

INDIAN NAME	ENGLISH NAME	BOTANICAL NAME
souf	aniseed	Pimpinella Anisum
seetul	allspice	Myrtus Pimenta
eelachie	cardamon	Elelbaria Cardamomum
jawatrie	mace	Myristica Moschata
jauphull	nutmeg	Myristica Moschata
kulmie darchini	cinnamon	Laurus Cinnamonum
dhunnia or kotimear	coriander	Doriandrum Sativum
laoong	cloves	Engenia Caryophyllata
zeera or jeera	cummin seed	Cummin Cyminum
kala mirchi	black pepper	Piper Nigrum
rai	mustard seed	Sinopis Chinesis

lal mirchi	chillies	*Capsicum Frutescens*
huldie	turmeric	*Curcuma Longa*
maythi	fenugreek	*Trigonella Foenum Craecum*
lassoon	garlic	*Alium Sativum*
sont	ginger (dry)	*Amomum Zingiber*
udruck	ginger (green)	*Amomum Zingiber*
khush-khush	poppy seed	*Papaver Somniferum*
pipel	long pepper	*Piper Longum*
hing	asafoetida	*Ferula Asafoetida*
chironji	chironji nut	*Buchanonia Latifolia*
badam	almond	*Amygdalia Communis*
nareul	coconut	*Cocus Nufifera*
keori or *kevara*	screw-pine	*Pandanus odoratissimus*

In addition to these, yogurt, coconut milk or cream, tamarind, and special legumes such as *channa* and *mussoor* are used in certain curries. Yogurt may be bought at many dairies, or it can be made at home. Tamarind and the pulses may be bought at shops that specialize in Indian spices (see page 62), and so may coconut milk or cream. But if preferred, this may be made at home.

The Indian method is to split a coconut in half and scrape away the flesh with a special grater. Place it in a saucepan with a large cup of water, and bring to the boil. Simmer for a minute, then pour into a stout china bowl and mash with a heavy spoon. Strain the liquor before use. This is known as 'thick milk'.

If the flesh is subjected once more to the same process—that is, boiled and strained, the liquid is known as 'thin milk'.

Another method is to mix or mash desiccated coconut in boiling water and then strain through fine muslin. Use approximately 1 breakfast cup of coconut to ½ pint of water.

Unless specifically instructed to do so, never place a lid on a saucepan in which a curry is being cooked with coconut milk, as the milk tends to curdle and the gravy turns lumpy.

In all the recipes given, the quantity of chilli has been reduced considerably, and if the curry is too pungent, it may be cut down still further. If curries have never been eaten before, it is also advisable to discard the seeds of red chillies.

NOTE: Throughout the book the term 'spoon' implies a FLAT, not a heaped, spoonful.

CHAPTER THREE

Dishes of Burma

NGA-BAUNG-DOKE

1 lb. cod or other white fish
1 tablespoon salt
½ teaspoon powdered turmeric
8 medium-sized onions
4 cloves garlic
1-inch piece of fresh ginger, or 1 teaspoon ground ginger
15–20 pieces of cabbage leaf— in Burma banana leaves are used

1–2 dried red chillies
1 tablespoon sessamum, mustard or other good cooking oil
1 tablespoon flour
1 tablespoon thick coconut milk (made from desiccated coconut—see page 11)
Toothpicks for pinning leaves

Clean the fish and rub thoroughly with half the mixed salt and turmeric; then cut into pieces 3 inches by 1½ inches.

Pound the chillies, garlic, ginger and 3 onions and add them to a paste made of the flour, coconut milk, oil and the remainder of the salt and turmeric. Slice the remainder of the onions very finely and mix into this.

Cut the cabbage leaves into 6-inch squares and on each square put a spoonful of paste, then a piece or two of fish; then some more paste and one or two pieces of fish. Fold the ends of the cabbage leaf and secure with a toothpick. Steam in a double boiler for 15–20 minutes.

An alternative method is to place the paste and fish on a nasturtium leaf and cover with another nasturtium leaf; and finally place the lot in a cabbage leaf and pin together with a toothpick.

In Burma banana leaves are used for the outer casing but any durable leaf which is edible may be used.

Enough for four.

SHA-NGA-BOUNG

1 lb. cod or other white fish
4 red chillies
6 cloves garlic
1 small stalk lemon grass (the white part)
The milk of 1 coconut, or the equivalent made from desiccated coconut—about ½ pint

1 teaspoon ground ginger or powdered ginger
3 onions, ground
1 tablespoon rice flour or cornflour
1 cup mustard, olive, sessamum or other good cooking oil
Salt to taste

Wash the fish, then bone and mince it.

Slice the chillies, remove the seeds, and soak in a tablespoon of water.

Now pound the chillies with the salt and other seasoning (leaving 1 onion) and mix with the fish and flour. The fish will now be in a thick paste, so mould it into cutlets.

Slice the remaining onion and fry it till light brown in the oil. Set it aside for garnish.

Then fry the fish cutlets till they are golden brown and cut them into slices.

Finally, pour the coconut milk into a pan, bring to the boil and put in the slices of fish. Put on a tight cover, lower the heat till the contents just simmer, and cook for 15 minutes.

Serve with rounds of fried onions on top and, if you wish, with some raw onions as well.

Enough for four.

FISH CURRY

In Burma this curry is usually made with *hilsa*—sable fish, a delicious fresh-water variety full of small bones, but as *hilsa* is not obtainable in Europe, any variety will do.

2–3 lb. fish
3 medium-sized onions
2 heads (*not* cloves) of garlic
½ inch (square) of root ginger
2–3 green chillies

1 cup vinegar
2 teaspoons salt
1 teaspoon powdered turmeric
¾ cup mustard oil

Clean the fish and rub thoroughly first with salt and then turmeric; then cut lengthwise in slices 1 inch wide and ¾ inch deep, and steep in vinegar for 12 hours.

Pound the onions, garlic and ginger into a paste. Boil the mustard oil, add the pounded ingredients and the whole chillies, stir well, put in the fish and cover with water. Simmer gently and feel from time to time with a fork or sharp knife, till the bones are soft.

Enough for six.

STEAMED FISH

1 lb. white fish
¼ coconut i.e. a coconut
    divided into 4
6 medium-sized onions
1 head of garlic

1 small bunch of lemon grass
1 small green chilli
9 squares of cabbage leaves
Toothpicks
Salt to taste

Clean and mince the raw fish. Extract 1 cup of milk from the coconut (directions on page 11). Chop the onions, garlic, lemon grass and chilli into small pieces and pound together.

Now mix the coconut milk, minced fish and seasoning and mould into finger-shaped rolls. Then wrap them in the cabbage-leaf squares, fasten each with a toothpick and steam for 15 minutes.

Enough for four.

SMOKED FISH

2½ lb. fine-textured fish
4 large onions
1½ oz. root ginger
1½ oz. garlic
1 tablespoon salt

2½ tablespoons malt vinegar
1 tablespoon saffron powder
1 tablespoon tomato sauce
14 oz. sessamum or mustard oil
10 long green chillies

Mix the salt and saffron powder and rub thoroughly into the cleaned fish. Cut the fish lengthwise into slices ¾ inch wide, and fry in the boiling oil. When done, drain and place the fish in a dish.

14

Slice the onions and fry till light brown. Drain and put them in another dish. Crush the ginger and garlic, drain off the juice and pour it on to the fish, together with the vinegar and tomato sauce. Mix gently, taking care not to break the fish.

Now place the fish in layers, sticking the chillies between the layers, and cover with fried onions; pour over this the fried oil. Cover and steam gently for 3-4 hours.

Enough for six.

BALACHAUNG

7 oz. dried prawns
11 oz. sessamum or mustard oil
1½ oz. shrimp paste (uncooked)

1 level teaspoon turmeric
1 onion
10 cloves garlic
1 inch of fresh root ginger
Salt to taste

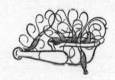

Pick and wash the prawns and pound them in a mortar. After peeling, slice the garlic, onion and ginger finely. Heat the oil till smoke rises from it and then fry separately the garlic, onion and ginger. Remove and place them in a dish. If added pungency is desired, grind 3 chillies and add them to the prawns.

Now mix the prawns with powdered turmeric and fry till crisp. Strain off oil. Stir the shrimp paste into such oil as clings to the pan and cook for 2 minutes. Then mix the prawns and cooked shrimp paste; add salt, garnish with the fried garlic, onion and ginger and serve with curry and rice.

The ingredients given should fill a 1-lb. bottle, and will keep for weeks, if not months.

PRAWN AND TOMATO CURRY

3–4 green chillies
14 oz. prawns
1 large onion
4 cloves garlic
1 teaspoon turmeric
4 tablespoons mustard or other cooking oil

2 tablespoons best Tavoy fish sauce (optional)
½ oz. coriander leaves
3 tomatoes, halved
1 cup water
Salt and pepper to taste

Grind the onion and garlic to a paste, and bring the oil to the boil. (Either ground-nut or mustard are the best oils for this dish.)

Fry the ground ingredients, turmeric, salt and pepper in the oil, and after cleaning the prawns, add them, together with the fish sauce (if used), coriander leaves, green chillies and tomatoes.

Now add the water and simmer till the prawns are cooked and the water has been absorbed, leaving a thick, rich gravy.

Enough for three.

CHICKEN KAUKSWE

A 3–4-lb. chicken
4 pints water
1 teaspoon ground saffron
4 cloves garlic
2 teaspoons powdered ginger or 2 slices of fresh ginger
4 chillies (optional)
½ cup vegetable oil

1 coconut from which 3 cups of milk should be extracted
1 tablespoon *dhall* flour (gram)
3½ lb. spaghetti
10 onions
Salt to taste

Quarter the chicken and rub the pieces thoroughly with saffron. Place in a pan with 4 pints of water and salt to taste, and bring the water to the boil. Then simmer till the flesh is tender.

Remove the chicken, strip the flesh from the bones and put it aside. Crack the bones and add them to the still simmering stock.

Now pound 9 onions, the garlic, ginger and chillies (if used) together and rub this mixture into the chicken meat. (The ingredients may be pounded in a mortar, ground on a *seel* [flat stone], or minced).

16

Heat the oil in a 2-quart saucepan till smoke rises, slice the remaining onion and brown it in the oil. Add the chicken and brown it also; then the stock, and simmer. Make a paste of the *dhall* flour and 1 cup of water, add it to the stock and simmer for 15 minutes; finally pour in the coconut milk and simmer for 10 minutes.

Boil the spaghetti in salt water till soft; drain away the water, put the spaghetti in a dish and pour the chicken over it. Serve with hard-boiled eggs cut into quarters, green (or 'spring') onions and sliced raw onions.

Enough for 8–10.

ROAST DUCK

1 duck of about 3–4 lb.	2 teaspoons salt
14 oz. pork	1 oz. dried mushrooms
2 eggs	5 large stalks of celery
3 oz. Chinese soy sauce	1 cup vegetable oil
1 oz. Chinese black sauce	1 length of sugar-cane, 12
7 medium-sized onions	inches long (optional)
15 cloves garlic	1 teaspoon pepper

Clean the duck thoroughly, then drain and dry it. Mix ½ teaspoon salt, ½ oz. Chinese black sauce and 1 oz. soy sauce and rub mixture over the duck, inside and out.

Mince the pork; chop the onions and 10 cloves of garlic; soak the mushrooms in hot water and then chop them. Chop the celery into 1-inch pieces.

Mix the above ingredients with the two eggs and add the remainder of the black sauce, soy sauce, salt, half the pepper and ½ cup of oil. This is the stuffing for the duck.

Stuff the duck and sew it. Then mash the remainder of the garlic, and mix in the rest of the pepper. Bring the remainder of the oil to the boil, add the garlic and pepper, remove from the stove, mix thoroughly and when still hot pour over the sugar-cane, which has been arranged at the bottom of a large dish. Sugar-cane is usually unobtainable in Britain, however; so merely pour the mixture into the dish, place the duck on top and roast for 1½ hours.

Enough for eight.

DUCK CURRY

1 duck of about 3–4 lb.
1 teaspoon powdered saffron
1 tablespoon salt
3 tablespoons Chinese soy sauce
10 medium-sized onions
1 inch of fresh ginger or 1 teaspoon ground ginger
15 cloves garlic
2–3 curry leaves or bay leaves
10 dried chillies—or less (this is optional)
5 peppercorns
1 cup vegetable or mustard oil

Clean the duck and cut it into 8 pieces. Rub thoroughly with salt, saffron and soy sauce and put it aside for an hour.

Grind or pound 5 of the onions with the ginger, about half the garlic and the chillies (if used).

Heat the oil till smoke rises and toss in the peppercorns, curry leaves and ground ingredients. Add the duck. Brown and simmer for 5 minutes. Then add sufficient water to cover the duck and no more. Simmer for 2 hours.

Slice the remaining onions and garlic and garnish the duck with them about half an hour before serving.

Serve hot.

Enough for eight.

COCONUT RICE

2½ cups rice (about 1¼ lb.)
1 coconut
2 teaspoons vegetable oil
½ teaspoon sugar
¼ teaspoon salt
1 onion

Grate the flesh of the coconut; soak in a cup of boiling water, and then squeeze the milk through thin muslin.

Wash the rice and place it in a pan with a thick bottom. Add the coconut milk to the rice till it is ¾ inch above it. Additional water might be needed.

Peel and quarter the onion and add to the rice; then put in the oil, sugar and salt. Mix well, then simmer till the liquid has evaporated and the rice is tender. Take out a grain or two and feel from time to time between finger and thumb.

Enough for four.

These recipes were kindly supplied by
MRS D. F. BYRNE
45 LANGLEY AVENUE
WORCESTER PARK
SURREY

CHAPTER FOUR

Dishes of Ceylon

BRINJAL POHIE

4 medium-sized *brinjals*
(aubergines)
1 tablespoon ground mustard
seed
¼ stem lemon grass
1 small sprig curry leaves
1 tablespoon pounded Mal-
dive fish (Bombay duck will
do)
4 cloves garlic, chopped
3 red chillies, sliced
2-inch stick of cinnamon
2-inch piece of *rampe**
20 dried chillies, pounded
(start with 2!)

1 tablespoon sugar
1 tablespoon coriander seed
1½ teaspoons ground white
cummin mixed with ½ tea-
spoon sweet cummin seed
1 tablespoon vinegar
1½ oz. tamarind squeezed in a
tablespoon of salt water
3 tablespoons coconut† or
other oil for frying, or
margarine
½ teacup thick coconut milk
About 1 teaspoon each of
ground saffron and salt
1 tablespoon sliced red onions

Slice the *brinjals*, rub the insides with the salt and saffron and fry in
oil or margarine.

Mix all the ground spices with the vinegar and tamarind in salt
water.

Heat 2 tablespoons of oil or fat in a pan and when very hot put
in the ground spices and other ingredients except the coconut milk
and sugar. Cook for 2–3 minutes, then add the *brinjals*, and finally
the coconut milk and sugar.

* *Rampe* or *rampa* is another name for screw-pine.

† Coconut oil is frequently used for cooking in Ceylon, Malaya, West
Africa and elsewhere, but it may not agree with Britons.

19

Bring to the boil and then simmer on a slow heat for 15–20 minutes, stirring gently, so as not to break up the *brinjals*.

Enough for four.

MISS BHADRANE DE SILVA
WAESNAGIRI
DEGODA LANE, AMCALANGODA
CEYLON

STUFFED CHILLI CURRY

6 large green capsicum chillies (these are not pungent)
¼ lb. red onions
2 oz. Maldive fish, pounded; or Bombay duck
¼ teaspoon chilli powder

1 dessertspoon lime juice
Salt to taste
2 tablespoons coconut oil, frying fat or unsalted margarine

Slit the chillies lengthwise about 2 inches from the tips. Remove pulp and seeds. Slice the red onions finely, mix with the rest of the ingredients, stuff the chillies with this mixture as well as the pulp and seeds that have been removed and fry in very hot oil or fat till brown.

Ingredients for the curry

1 cup thick coconut milk, or cow's milk
1 teaspoon ground chilli
1 teaspoon Maldive fish or Bombay duck

4 red onions
1 sprig curry leaves
A pinch of saffron
2 teaspoons lemon juice
Salt to taste

Slice the red onions, mix with the other ingredients and pour into a saucepan. Then add the stuffed chillies. Place pan on the stove, bring to the boil and then simmer for 10–15 minutes.

In Ceylon a little curry powder is sprinkled over the dish just before it is removed from the stove, but this is not recommended, as the treatment makes it somewhat too harsh for European palates.

Enough for three.

MRS H. A. PERARA
EXCISE BUNGALOW
MATARA
CEYLON

20

EGG STEW

4 eggs
4 medium-sized potatoes, sliced
2 medium-sized onions, chopped
1 tablespoon green chillies, sliced thinly
⅔ teaspoon powdered turmeric or saffron
2 tablespoons pickling onions, sliced thinly
2 sprigs *karapincha* (curry leaves)
4 1-inch pieces of *rampe* (or screw-pine) or lemon grass

1-inch piece of ginger
1-inch stick of cinnamon
3 cups water
1 clove garlic
1 tablespoon flour
2 cloves
5 cardamoms
25 peppercorns
3 tablespoons Maldive fish, powdered (Bombay duck will do)
1 tablespoon vinegar
3 tablespoons coconut oil or butter
Salt to taste

Grind the cloves, cardamoms and peppercorns together. Whisk the eggs and add 1 tablespoon sliced pickling onions, 1 tablespoon sliced green chillies, pinch of salt, 1 tablespoon powdered fish and half of the ground cloves, cardamoms and pepper. Mix well, pour into a pudding basin and steam for 30 minutes, then cut into 4 or 6 pieces and set aside.

Place the sliced potatoes in a bowl and add 3 cups of water, 1 tablespoon flour, 1 tablespoon vinegar, ⅔ teaspoon turmeric (or saffron), 1 tablespoon sliced pickling onions, 2 pieces of *rampe* (screw-pine) or lemon grass, 1 sprig of curry leaves, 2 tablespoons ground fish, the cinnamon, garlic, ginger, remainder of the ground seasoning, and salt.

Heat the coconut oil (or butter) in a thick pan and in it fry the medium-sized chopped onions, 2 pieces of lemon grass (or *rampe*, etc.) and a sprig of curry leaves for 2 minutes. Add the potato mixture to the fried ingredients and cover the pan. When cooked, put in pieces of the steamed egg mixture, simmer for 5 minutes and remove from the stove and serve.

Enough for four.

MISS ESTHER APONSO
WINIFRED ESTATE
DIVULAPITIYA
CEYLON

FRIED POTATOES

This dish bears no resemblance to chipped potatoes or fried potatoes done in the English way.

3 large potatoes
1 large Spanish onion
2 teaspoons powdered
   Maldive fish or Bombay
   duck

2 teaspoons chilli powder
1 sprig curry leaves or bay
   leaves
1 tablespoon dripping
Salt to taste

Boil the potatoes in their jackets after first scrubbing them well. Peel and cut them into small pieces. Add to them half the chilli powder and some salt and set on one side.

Cut the large onion into thin slices; add the remaining chilli powder and salt to these and mix well.

Now heat the dripping in a frying-pan and add the sliced onion and curry leaves. Fry till the onion is soft; then add potatoes and fry all together, stirring all the time. Just before removing from the stove, add the powdered fish.

The entire operation should not take more than 20–25 minutes.

Enough for four.

MRS DAVID THOMPSON
ROBGILL GROUP
BOGAWANTALAWA
CEYLON

CHICKEN CURRY

1 large chicken
2 teaspoons chilli powder
1 teaspoon curry powder
   cloves garlic
-inch stick of cinnamon
1 sprig celery
8 cloves
1-inch piece of *rampa*
   (optional)
1 large sprig curry leaves (or
   bay leaves)

1 green chilli, sliced
2 slices of green ginger
$1\frac{1}{2}$ cups thin coconut milk
$\frac{1}{2}$ cup thick coconut milk
1 dessertspoon pickling
   onions, sliced
1 dessertspoon dripping or
   any cooking fat
$\frac{1}{2}$ teaspoon fenugreek
Salt to taste
Juice of 2 limes or lemons

Cut the chicken into neat joints and season with salt, curry powder and chilli powder. Heat the dripping in a large saucepan and when it is very hot crush 3 cloves of garlic and toss them in. Fry till brown. Now add half the fenugreek and also fry till brown; after which add the sliced onions, *rampa* (if used), green chilli, celery (cut into large bits), cinnamon, curry leaves (or bay), and fry till the onions are golden brown. At this stage, put in the chicken and fry, stirring all the time. When the pieces of chicken are brown, add the thin coconut milk and cloves, the green ginger and the remaining fenugreek and garlic, cut into tiny pieces.

Stir well, cover the pan with a snugly fitting lid and simmer gently till the chicken is tender, after which add the thick coconut milk and lime (or lemon) juice. Stir well and simmer slowly till the gravy thickens, but be sure NOT to cover the pan after adding the thick coconut milk.

Enough for four.

MRS DAVID THOMPSON

HOT STEW WITH RICE

2 lb. mutton
1 lb. fine-grained rice, such as Patna, Burma or Kashmir
6 gills water or stock
4 tablespoons ghee, margarine, or equivalent cooking fat or oil
2 oz. red onions
2 teaspoons powdered black pepper
1 teaspoon curry powder
¼ lb. raisins
¼ lb. chopped cashew nuts
¼ lb. cooked green peas
½ teacup thick coconut milk
¼ teaspoon mixed powdered spices—cloves, cardamoms, cinnamon
A pinch of ground garlic
A pinch of powdered ginger
1-inch piece of *rampe* (optional)
Salt to taste

Wash the rice well in warm water and place it in a thick pan with stock or water, and salt to taste. Stock may be made by boiling the mutton in 6 gills of water. Boil rice.

When the rice is soft, but with each grain firm and separate from the others, press it into a rice mould in the form of a ring that has been greased with ghee or margarine. Then turn it into a large fireproof dish or casserole.

23

Heat the fat or ghee in a frying-pan; slice the onions and brown them, together with the *rampe*, if used. Put in the mutton, cut up in cubes, and braise.

Now stir the ground ingredients into the coconut milk, add this to the mutton, bring to the boil and simmer for 5 minutes, or until soft.

Remove the *rampe*, then place the cooked mutton in the centre of the rice ring. Make a little gravy with flour, egg and seasoning and pour it over the meat. Sprinkle the rice with the raisins, cashew nuts and peas and put the dish in a slow oven for 20 minutes.

Enough for 6–8.

MRS J. J. EVIJESEKERA
MONROVIA GROUP
DODANDUWA
CEYLON

MOLOGOTHANNIE

1 lb. beef
10 peppercorns
2-inch stick of cinnamon
1 large onion
1 large, ripe tomato
1 piece of *rampe* leaf
½ dessertspoon ground coriander
6–8 cups water
½ dessertspoon ghee or dripping
1 piece of *sera* leaf (or bay can be used)

1 sprig curry leaves
A pinch of saffron or turmeric
3 cloves garlic
1 inch of ginger
1 teacup milk
½ dessertspoon white cinnamon
8 red onions, sliced
1 dessertspoon ground chillies
2 teaspoons curry powder

Boil the beef with the peppercorns, cinnamon, tomato, large onion, coriander, *rampe*, *sera* and curry leaves, garlic, ginger, 4 red onions and 2 quarts water.

When meat is tender, add saffron (or turmeric) and ground chillies, mixed into a paste with the milk. Boil for 5 minutes, then simmer.

Slice the remainder of the red onions finely, fry in ghee (or dripping) and mix in, stirring thoroughly. Simmer gently for 10 minutes, strain and eat with rice and chutney or lime pickle.

Half a dessertspoon of ground chilli will make this dish much too pungent for European palates; so half a TEAspoonful is advised at first. If you like it hotter, add more the next time.

Enough for four.

MISS PEARL DE SILVA
'MARYLANDS'
MORUPOLA ESTATE
GAMPAHA, WP, CEYLON

SATHÉ CURRY

Seasoning and Spices

- 1 *rounded* teaspoon raw curry powder
- ½ level teaspoon powdered pepper
- ¼ level teaspoon chilli powder
- ¼ level teaspoon powdered cinnamon
- ⅛ level teaspoon powdered cloves
- ⅛ level teaspoon powdered cardamom
- A pinch of *powdered* ginger (sweet)
- 1 level teaspoon *ground** ginger
- 1 level teaspoon garlic (crushed)
- 1 dessertspoon vinegar
- Salt to taste

Also:

- 1 lb. beef, roasted or boiled and cut into 16 1-inch cubes
- 5 tablespoons coconut oil, salad oil, butter or margarine
- 24 whole, small red onions
- 1½ cups coconut milk, fresh cow's milk or unsweetened tinned milk
- 1 *rounded* teaspoon cornflour or rice flour
- 2-inch piece of *rampe*
- ⅛ level teaspoon turmeric powder
- 3 green chillies, sliced
- 12 red onions
- 1 sprig curry, bay or marjoram leaves
- Juice of 1 large lime or lemon
- Salt to taste
- Metal or thin wooden skewers for threading beef, etc.

Mix the beef thoroughly with the seasoning ingredients and spices, and allow to marinade for 1 hour. Skewer beef and red onions alternately: 4 cubes of beef and 3 onions.

Heat 3 tablespoons of fat in a heavy, shallow pan and braise

---

* Ground ginger is stick or root ginger which has been pounded or ground, and it contains some juice. Powdered ginger is the dried root ground into powder and has no juice in it.

beef for 20–30 minutes, and when well browned remove from the pan and arrange on a flat meat dish.

Pour the remainder of the fat into another pan and when hot add curry leaves, *rampe*, the remaining 12 red onions and green chillies. When the onions are golden, add the cornflour, coconut milk and turmeric powder. Stir well, add salt and lime or lemon juice, and when the sauce has cooked thoroughly, remove *rampe* and curry leaves and pour over beef.

Sathé Curry may be garnished by cutting 4 ripe, red chillies lengthwise from tip to stalk. Retain the stems but remove seeds and inner pith. Drop the chillies into iced water and chill for 2 hours, when the chillies will open into lovely flowers. Arrange them on the dish with a few sprigs of parsley or other herbs.

Enough for four.

MISS IRIS MUNASINGHE
15 APONSO AVENUE
DEHIWELA
CEYLON

BEEF CURRY

2 lb. beef	20 dried chillies
¼ lb. onions	2 teaspoons coriander seed
1 clove garlic	10 cardamoms
1-inch piece of greenginger	1-inch stick of cinnamon
2-inch piece of *rampe* or bay leaf	Milk from ½ coconut, about ½ pint
2-inch piece of *sera* or curry leaf	Salt and vinegar to taste
	2 tablespoons vegetable oil

Cut the beef into 1-inch cubes, put into a bowl and mix with the salt, vinegar and curry powder.

Curry powder: this is made by pounding 20 dried chillies, 2 teaspoons coriander, 10 cardamoms, 1-inch stick of cinnamon, and then roasting them till they give off a strong odour.

Let the beef and spices marinade for half an hour. Then heat the oil and fry the sliced onions, garlic and ginger till brown. Put in the meat and spices in the liquid and brown. Add *rampe* and *sera* leaves and cook till the liquid is absorbed. Then put in the coconut milk and cook again till the beef is tender and the gravy thick.

Enough for four.

MRS VYVETTE LOOS
'KINGSTON'
NEGOMBO
CEYLON

OX-HEART BLACK CURRY

Clean, slice and soak the heart in about ½ pint vinegar while you get together the following ingredients:

2 cloves garlic, sliced
4 1-inch slices of ginger
10 onions, finely sliced
2 cloves, powdered
1-inch stick of cinnamon
6 cardamoms, powdered
1 cup grated coconut
1 tablespoon coriander seed
6 curry leaves
1 teaspoon white cummin seed
½ teaspoon sweet cummin seed

12 dried red chillies
1 dessertspoon fat, ghee, butter or cooking oil
1 piece of lemon grass
1 piece of *rampe* leaf
1 teaspoon fennel
1 tablespoon small onions
Juice of 1½ limes or lemons
2 cups water
1 teaspoon sugar
Salt to taste

Add the cloves, garlic, ginger, sliced onions, cinnamon and cardamoms to the vinegar in which the heart is soaking.

Roast till dark brown the grated coconut; then grind the coriander seed, curry leaves, white cummin, sweet cummin, and 12 red chillies together and add to the roasted coconut. Mix well.

Put 1 dessertspoon of fat into a thick pan, add the lemon grass, *rampe* leaf, fennel and the tablespoon of small onions. When brown, add the sliced meat, etc., salt, browned coconut and other ingredients. Mix well, add 2 cups of water and the juice of the lemons or limes, bring to the boil and simmer till the heart is quite soft.

Before removing from the stove, mix in 1 teaspoon of sugar.

Enough for at least four.

MRS VYVETTE LOOS

SPICY CEYLONESE PORK CURRY

1 liver (pig's)	1 teaspoon white cummin seed
1½ lb. pork (lean and fat mixed)	8 peppercorns
	½-inch piece of turmeric
2 large onions	2-inch stick of cinnamon
12 red chillies	6 cloves
6 cloves garlic	1 tablespoon sweet oil
1 inch of ginger	Vinegar

Parboil pork and liver and cut both into tiny cubes. Grind all the spices in a little strong vinegar.

Put the oil into a frying-pan and fry pork and liver till brown. Some of the fat from the pork will melt. Drain this away into a receptacle, leaving only a trace in the pan. Chop the onions and fry in this remaining fat, and when cooked, add them to the pork and liver.

Now wash the pan, add the ground spices and salt to the meat, etc., return to the pan and mix thoroughly.

Simmer over a low flame till tender. Add a tablespoon of vinegar, 3 chillies and a stalk of curry leaves as garnish.

Enough for 6–8.

MRS VYVETTE LOOS

VERY YOUNG MILK SHARK CURRY

This exotic-sounding dish was once beyond the reach of people in Britain, but now that sharks are caught off Cornish waters, some of the luckier ones may indulge in this concoction. If you can't get hold of shark, cod will do. If shark is used, skin it.

1 baby shark, 12–15 inches long, or cod

For every 2 lb. fish use:

4 cloves garlic, chopped	1 sprig curry leaves
3 slices of green ginger, chopped	1-inch stick of cinnamon
	1 tablespoon coriander seed
2-inch piece of *rampe* leaf	1 teaspoon white cummin seed

½-inch stem lemon grass

Roast and powder these ingredients. You will also need:

2 cloves garlic
2 1-inch slices of ginger
1-inch stick of cinnamon
5–6 curry leaves
10 cardamoms, powdered
Juice of 2 limes or lemons
1 dessertspoon ghee or
cooking oil
2 1-inch pieces of turmeric

½ teaspoon sweet cummin
seed

½ teaspoon chopped fennel
leaves
Milk of 1 coconut
½ teaspoon ground saffron
20 dried chillies (roasted
dark and ground)
1 dessertspoon tamarind
juice
Salt to taste

Place the first batch of ingredients into a thick pan and fry in a little fat till dark brown.

Mix the second batch—except the tamarind juice—with the fish, and cook in the fat. When fried, add the first batch of ingredients, mix thoroughly, simmer with the added tamarind juice and salt to taste.

Do not boil. Simmer and remove from the pan when the fish is soft and flaky.

When the fish is done, one should add a spoon of arrack. As arrack is not generally available in Europe, however, use rum; but this last stage is optional.

If shark, enough for six. If cod, enough for four.

MRS VYVETTE LOOS

FISH CURRY

2 lb. fish
1 dessertspoon mustard oil
or cooking oil
10 onions, sliced
4 cloves garlic, sliced
4 1-inch slices of ginger

1 dessertspoon ground
mustard
½ teaspoon saffron
2–3 fennel leaves, chopped
½ teaspoon ground or
powdered chilli

1 piece of *rampe* leaf, *sera*   1 dessertspoon jaggery,*
    leaf or 2–3 curry leaves   'foot' sugar, or 'pieces'
Vinegar and salt to taste

Skin, wash and cut the fish into pieces. Put it into a pan, add a little water, vinegar and salt to taste. Boil for 5 minutes, remove from the stove.

Heat the oil and brown the sliced onions, garlic, ginger, and *rampe*, *sera* or curry leaves.

Add the remainder of the spices, fish and the liquor (water and vinegar) and boil for 10 minutes without covering. Just before removing, add the jaggery or sugar. This gives it a distinctive tang.

This fish curry should be served with lime pickle.

Enough for four.

MRS VYVETTE LOOS

CRAB CURRY

5 large crabs   6 green chillies
3 cups thin coconut milk   2 dessertspoons ground chillies
2 cups thick coconut milk   (try *tea*spoons first!)
2 handfuls *murunga* leaves   1 sprig curry leaves
6 red onions   1 dessertspoon coconut oil,
Juice of 1 lemon   ghee, butter or margarine
Salt to taste

Wash the crabs well and place the edible portions in a thick saucepan. Slice the onions and brown them in the oil or fat. Add them with the coconut milk and the other ingredients to the crab, bring to the boil and simmer till the crab meat is tender. Cook till the gravy is reduced to no less than 4 cups.

If the crabs are very large and the hard shell has to be split, salvage the juice that runs out, and use it in the cooking.

Enough for six.

MRS N. REGINALD
HARROW ESTATE
PUNDULAYA
CEYLON

* Jaggery is palm sugar, made from the sap or juice of the palm. If it can't be obtained, ask your grocer for 'foot' sugar, which is very black and has a rich, treacly smell, or for 'pieces' (Barbadoes sugar).

CHAPTER FIVE

Dishes of India and Pakistan

THE cuisine of India and Pakistan has been very fully dealt with in *Curries of India* and *The Second Book of Curries*, and therefore only a few recipes have been included here.

INDIA

SERPATHALA

1 pint pig's blood	12 cloves, ground
1 pig's heart and liver and ¼ lb. pork	1 oz. tamarind
	½ teaspoon salt
4 oz. ghee or mustard oil	½ teaspoon ground saffron or turmeric
6 dried chillies, ground	
½ teaspoon ground black pepper	8–10 small onions
	5 oz. best malt vinegar
½–1 teaspoon ground cummin	6 green chillies
¼–½ teaspoon ground cinnamon	¼ teaspoon ground ginger
	6 cloves garlic

Place the tamarind in a bowl, cover with boiling water and soak for an hour, then put it into a cheese-cloth or fine muslin and squeeze out the juice.

Boil the pig's blood till it turns black; then boil the pig's heart, liver and pork, with the salt; then cut them up and fry them in 2 oz. fat or oil, together with the saffron or turmeric.

Now slice the onions finely and brown them in 2 oz. of fat. Drain off the fat and in it fry the dried chillies, pepper, cummin, 3 cloves of garlic (mashed), cloves and cinnamon. Add these to the onions.

Put these spices and onions into a thick pan, pour in the vinegar and tamarind juice; add the fried liver, etc., blood, the remainder of the garlic, ginger and green chillies chopped into small pieces. Cover the vessel and simmer for an hour, or until such time as the gravy is thick. To be eaten with rice.

Enough for four.

VEGETABLE PILAU

- 1 breakfast cup fine rice—Patna, Kashmiri or Burma
- 4 medium-sized carrots, peeled and sliced
- ½ breakfast cup cauliflower heads
- ¾ cup fresh shelled peas
- 5 tablespoons seedless raisins or sultanas
- 2 large onions, sliced
- 2 tablespoons butter, ghee or margarine
- 4–6 bay leaves
- 1 teaspoon salt
- ¾ cup peanuts, almonds, pine kernels, pistachios or cashew nuts

Wash the rice and soak it for an hour.

Place the peas, carrots and cauliflower in 4 breakfast cups of water in a thick saucepan, put on the lid and boil till tender but *not soft*; then strain off the water and keep for stock.

Heat the fat and fry half the sliced onions as well as the nuts till golden brown, then remove them from the pan.

Put the cooked vegetables into the remainder of the hot fat, mix them well but take care not to break them up. Do not brown them. After they have been mixed with the fat, remove them and set them aside.

Now put the rice, that has been drained, into the pan with the hot ghee or fat, add the raisins or sultanas, simmer and stir for a couple of minutes, then pour in the stock, add salt and the bay leaves.

Bring to the boil, then turn down the heat and simmer till the rice is done and the stock absorbed.

Mix the rice and cooked vegetables together, empty into a serving dish and garnish with remainder of onions, fried crisply, and nuts.

Other vegetables, in season, may be used.

Enough for four.

½ lb. *m.* *ll* (these lentils
may be bought at any shop
which sells Indian spices)
¼ lb. ghee or butter
4 teaspoons ground onions
1 teaspoon ground chillies
½ teaspoon ground turmeric

½ teaspoon ground ginger
¼ teaspoon ground garlic
1 teaspoon salt (more, if
needed, to be added after
cooking)
6 onions, finely sliced

Place the *dhall* in a thick pan and brown it, mixing the while with a wooden spoon. When slightly browned, put in salt and all the ground condiments and add enough water to rise 2 inches above them. If you have boiling water handy, use it, as this helps to break up the *dhall* quickly. Boil till the *dhall* is quite dissolved. Don't mix it with a spoon, but allow it to cake.

When the *dhall* is well dissolved, whisk it. In India this is done with a wooden instrument called a *ghootnee*, but a wire whisk will serve as well.

Warm the ghee or butter in a separate pan, put in the sliced onions and fry till dark brown and then mix into the churned *dhall*; then pour *dhall* and onions into the remains of the melted ghee in which the onions were fried.

Mix well, place a well-fitting cover on the pan and simmer for 15 minutes. To be eaten with either rice, or rice and curry.

Enough for four.

PAKISTAN

SHAMI KABAB or CABOB

1 lb. mince (very fine)
2 small onions cut into pieces
½ cup *channa dhall* or split peas
4 cloves

4 cardamoms
8 black peppercorns
1 egg
Salt to taste

This is a very simple but tasty dish.

Place all the ingredients except the egg in a thick-bottomed pan, cover with water and boil gently till the water has evaporated and the mixture is thick, and the meat tender.

Now mix in one raw, beaten egg, pass the mixture through a mincer and allow to cool.

Finally, mould the mixture into small, flat cakes and fry on either side till brown.

Enough for four.

Shami Kabab may be eaten with rice or bread, but it goes best with either *chappattis* or *parattas*, and should be accompanied with either chilli, tomato and beet pickle; lime pickle; or merely raw green chillies. The last, would, however, prove much too fiery for the average British palate and one is advised to treat raw green chillies with great respect until the palate is accustomed to them. The eating of food that is too pungent has put many an experimenter off curries for good.

CHICKEN KORMA

1 roasting chicken, about 2 lb., cut into pieces
½ lb. butter or ghee
1 medium-sized onion
½ teaspoon ground saffron or turmeric
3 teaspoons ground coriander seed

½ teaspoon ground chilli
½ teaspoon mashed garlic
1 5-oz. bottle plain yogurt
1-inch piece of ginger, sliced
1 teaspoon each of cloves, black pepper and cummin seed, whole
Salt to taste

Slice the onion finely, brown in the butter and then place in a small dish. Put the ground spices into a breakfast cup of water, add to the fat in the pan and cook for 3 minutes, stirring the while. Now add the chicken, mix well, see that the meat is just covered by water and boil for 20 minutes with the lid on the pan.

When the liquid has almost evaporated, continue to cook, but stir the chicken till golden brown.

Crush the browned onion with a spoon and add it to the chicken with the yogurt, salt to taste and remainder of the spices. Add a cup of water, put on the lid and simmer gently till the chicken is tender. If the chicken is not quite done and the liquid has evaporated, add a little more water and cook for a further period.

The entire process should take about 1½ hours.

Enough for six.

CHAPTER SIX

Dishes of Indonesia and Thailand

INDONESIA

THE main dishes in Indonesia consist usually of rice and fish, chicken, meat and vegetables. The Indonesian *consommé*, or *soto*, is very popular all over Java and Madura. Sometimes it is consumed as a main dish, with either boiled or steamed rice.

SOTO AJAM

1 chicken	2 leeks, cooked
1 large onion, finely sliced	2 medium-sized potatoes,
3 cloves garlic, finely sliced	peeled
1 large tablespoon mustard	1 dessertspoon lemon juice,
oil or cooking oil	a pinch of red pepper
½ teaspoon ground ginger	(optional)
2 eggs	Salt and pepper to taste
2 large carrots, cooked	4 meat cubes (optional)
2 sticks celery	

Cut the chicken into pieces. Fry the onion and garlic to a golden colour, then boil the chicken till tender, with the onion, garlic, ginger and salt and pepper, in enough water to cover it—about 1 quart.

Hard-boil the eggs, slice them and cut the slices into halves. Slice the peeled potatoes and fry them; chop the carrots into small cubes and slice the celery and leeks finely.

To serve, put into each *bouillon* cup or bowl a piece of chicken, a few pieces of egg, some fried potato, onion, garlic, carrot, celery and leek. Then pour hot chicken broth into each cup and serve at once. If added flavour is desired, make a sauce by dissolving 4 meat cubes in boiling water and flavouring with a dessertspoon of lemon juice and a pinch of red pepper.

Enough for 4–6.

M. JUSUF RONODIPURO
PRESS AND CULTURAL ATTACHÉ
KEDUTAAN BESAR REPUBLIK OF INDONESIA
38 GROSVENOR SQUARE
LONDON, W1

SATE AJAM—one version

1 chicken	1 meat cube dissolved in a
Some metal skewers	little boiling water
1 teaspoon ground black pepper	Juice of 1 lemon
1 red chilli, steamed till tender	1 cup ketchup
3 cloves garlic, fried	Salt to taste
4 tablespoons peanut butter	

Pound together the red chilli, garlic and peanut butter and mix into a sauce with the lemon juice and the meat cube dissolved in boiling water.

Cut the chicken into small pieces and thread these on to the skewers. Mix the black pepper, salt and ketchup and pour the mixture over the chicken, and steam till the chicken is tender. Then grill on the skewers and serve with the sauce. Add more lemon juice if needed.

Enough for four.

SATE AJAM—another version

2-lb. chicken or 1 lb. mutton	1 large clove garlic
2 walnuts	Juice of 1 lemon or 1
1 onion	teaspoon tamarind juice
1-inch piece of ginger	Salt

Cut the chicken (boned) or mutton into 1-inch pieces. Mix the remainder of the ingredients together with a pinch of salt; then grind or crush them. Rub mixture thoroughly into the chicken or meat and allow it to stand for an hour.

Sate or Sauce

½ cup roasted peanuts	1½ dessertspoons thick
1 green chilli	Japanese soy sauce

1 small onion
1 onion sliced finely
Salt to taste

1 tablespoon cooking oil
(coconut)
Juice of 1 lime or lemon

Fry the sliced onion brown and put on one side. Remove the thin red skin from the peanuts and grind them. Grind the chilli and small onion together and fry them in hot coconut oil. After 3 minutes, add the peanuts and salt. The fried mixture will be thick, so add a little warm water and make into a smooth sauce.

Now remove from the stove, mix in the soy sauce and lemon juice and pour over the chicken. Sprinkle fried onion over the dish and serve.

Enough for four.

AJAM PANGGANG

1 chicken
1-inch piece of ginger
1-inch piece of saffron or
    turmeric or ½ teaspoon
    ground saffron or
    ground turmeric
Salt to taste

1 large clove garlic
2 medium-sized onions
3 green chillies
Milk of 1 coconut, about ½
    pint
Small piece of lemon grass
1 saffron leaf

Split the chicken along the line of the breast. Grind the ginger, garlic, onions, chillies, saffron or turmeric and mix thoroughly. Add the coconut milk and salt and mix again. Pour into a thick-bottomed pan, toss in the lemon grass and saffron leaf and bring to the boil.

Now put in the chicken and gently stir the liquid while turning the chicken, and simmer slowly till every drop of the milk evaporates.

Finally, remove the chicken from the pan and brown *very gently* under a grill for 1½ hours.

In Indonesia this operation is conducted over a charcoal fire which gives out a slow, steady heat, but as the normal housewife does not cook over charcoal, the grill will have to suffice.

Enough for four.

OTAK-OTAK

2 tablespoons olive oil
2 trout (or other fresh-water
    fish)
¼ teaspoon coriander seeds,
    ground

1 egg
½ cup milk
4 tomatoes
1 small lettuce
1–2 strips of red pepper

1 large onion, chopped   Pepper and salt to taste
4 cloves garlic, chopped   Some cabbage leaves

Wash the fish and beat gently with the back of a heavy wooden spoon or a meat-beater to loosen the skin; then carefully remove the flesh with as little damage to the skin as possible. Remove all bones from the flesh, and chop it finely.

Mix the flesh with the coriander, onion, garlic, egg, milk, chopped onion, pepper, and salt.

Fill both fish skins with this stuffing, secure, then wrap each fish in cabbage leaves and steam for 20 minutes.

Finally, fry the fish brown in olive oil and serve garnished with small pieces of red pepper, tomato and lettuce. Parsley may also be used for garnishing, or water cress.

Enough for four.

M. JUSUF RONODIPURO

NASI KUNING (Yellow Rice)

3 cups milk   A few celery leaves
1 teaspoon turmeric powder   2 red peppers
1 bay leaf   ½ small cucumber
½ teaspoon salt   1 large onion
2 cups rice   2 eggs

Add the turmeric, bay leaf and salt to the milk and bring it to the boil. Then remove the bay leaf. Wash rice and stir milk into it. Cook till the milk is absorbed, then steam till the rice is dry.

Cut the red peppers into flower shapes, the cucumber into slices, fry the onion in rings and make the eggs into an omelette, and cut into strips.

Turn the rice out into a large dish and garnish with the celery leaves, red peppers, cucumber, onion rings and strips of omelette.

Enough for two.

M. JUSUF RONODIPURO

SERIKAYA

3 eggs	1 cup milk
1 vanilla pod (or less), powdered	3 bananas
1 cup sugar	

Beat the vanilla into the eggs, add the sugar and milk and stir the mixture well.

Now add the bananas, sliced, pour the mixture into a deep basin or dish and steam or bake gently for 20–30 minutes till set.

Enough for two.

M. JUSUF RONODIPURO

THAILAND

RAMA'S BATH

1 lb. beef	1 lump of palm sugar or 1
1 lb. grated coconut	large teaspoon 'foot' or
7 dried red chillies (try 2	Barbadoes sugar see note
for a start!)	to page 30
4 shallots	5 teaspoons roasted peanuts
4 large cloves garlic	2½ tablespoons flour
1½ inches of ginger	1 lb. spinach or the
Small stalk lemon grass	equivalent of spring greens
½ teaspoon salt	Cream or yogurt
Soy sauce	

Wash the beef and slice it into strips. Boil the coconut in a pint of water, allow it to cool, strain the 'cream', and put aside.

Boil the beef in the remainder of the coconut milk, and when it

comes to the boil, simmer it with a little soy sauce, sugar and peanuts ground or pounded coarsely.

Pound the shallots, chillies, garlic, ginger, lemon grass, and salt together and mix into a sauce with the 'cream' from the coconut milk. Add the boiled beef, sauce, sugar, etc.; make a thin paste of the flour with a little cold water, and pour over the concoction. Bring to the boil, stirring, put on a close-fitting lid, and simmer till the beef is tender.

The greens should be boiled very rapidly in a little salted water for not more than 8–10 minutes; then drain off the water, arrange the greens on a dish, place the beef on top and crown with 2 teaspoons of cream or a bottle of yogurt.

This should always be eaten with rice. (Don't throw away the water from the greens, but use it as stock.)

Enough for four.

DOVE or WOOD-PIGEON

1 large dove or wood-pigeon	1 dessertspoon sugar
1 small cucumber	A few crushed coriander leaves
1 small onion, sliced	
1 large clove garlic, sliced	1 dessertspoon flour
3 green chillies	1 tablespoon lard
1 tablespoon best wine vinegar or ¼ pint cider	2 dessertspoons Chinese soy sauce
Salt to taste	

Dismember the pigeon, and slice the cucumber, preferably without peeling it. The best cucumbers are NOT the thick ones, but those that are thin and very dark green. These are succulent, whereas the large, light-green or yellowish cucumbers are tough and packed with seeds.

Slice the green chillies, remove the seeds, and cut them into diamond shapes.

Mix together the vinegar (or cider), salt, sugar, soy sauce and flour.

Fry the garlic till golden brown, add the bird and stir for 2 minutes. Then put in the other ingredients (except chillies and coriander) and the blended liquid and stir again. When the bird is tender serve in a dish with the chopped coriander leaves and green chillies on top. Dove or wood-pigeon is eaten with rice.

Farmers, who consider pigeons a nuisance and shoot them, might relish them served this way.

One bird to each person.

CHAPTER SEVEN

Dishes of Iran and Iraq

IRAN

IRAN is the name by which Persia is known officially in the West today, but it is the name by which Persia has always been known to Persians. Their cuisine has much in common with all food in the East but, like Turkish cookery, pungent spices are not used as heavily as in India, Pakistan, Ceylon, Burma, Indonesia and Malaya.

POLO

This has no connection with the game of the same name, which, incidentally, was invented in Persia (Iran).

Wash 1 breakfast cup of rice twice in warm water and place in a bowl with *warm* water. Put into the bowl ½ teaspoon of salt in a cotton or muslin bag—it is important that the salt does not touch the rice. Leave for 24 hours. Then drain in a colander and tip the rice into a panful of boiling water. After 15 minutes test a few grains of rice between finger and thumb, and when tender, remove from the heat, drain and put into a dish.

Now place a knob of butter on the bottom of a pan, add about ½ pint of water and boil. Pour half the liquid away, leaving ¼ pint of the oily mixture at the bottom of the pan. Add the rice to this and cook fast till steam rises; this should happen in a matter of seconds. Then drain off the liquid through the rice.

Decrease the heat almost to vanishing point, wrap the lid of the pan in cloth to prevent the steam from escaping and cook gently for 30 minutes. The *polo* is now ready to serve.

Enough for two.

Polo can also be made with the addition of: lentils (*Addas Polo*); broad beans (*Baghela Polo*); kidney beans (*Loubia Polo*); vermicelli (*Reshteh Polo*); and black cherries (*Albalu Polo*).

For the first four, prepare the *polo* as above. Boil the alternative ingredients in a separate pan with salt to taste; then add the *polo* to the ingredient, or ingredients, and mix thoroughly, before the final steaming. At that stage also, onions, garlic, a little saffron or turmeric, paprika or other spices may be added (never sweet spices); but this is optional.

If fresh or dried cherries are used, boil and mix with sugar (sugar should be a little less than a tenth of the weight of cherries) and add a little vanilla. When the cherries are tender, put half the *polo* in the serving dish, then half the cherries, then the remainder of the *polo* and the rest of the cherries on top. Add the syrup.

If cherries are used, no other spices should be added.

Polo made with vegetables is a dish on its own, though it can be accompanied by mutton or chicken.

TAHCHIN BAREH (Lamb) and TAHCHIN ESFENADJ (Spinach)

Prepare a dish of *polo* as instructed in the preceding recipe, but in the second stage, when boiling a knob of butter and a little water in a pan, do not drain off the butter–water but add the rice to it.

Take 1 lb. lamb, either from the saddle or leg, remove all fat and boil in water to cover till tender, adding salt only when the water *comes* to the boil. Then drain the water into a dish, cut the meat into cubes, put into the *polo* pan with a knob of butter and a little water, add the *polo*, cook gently for 30 minutes, and then pour in the stock in which the meat was cooked.

Boil 1 lb. spinach very fast for 8 minutes in just the water that clings to it after it has been washed and drained. Put half in the bottom of a serving dish, then the rice and meat, and finally the rest of the spinach on top.

Here again, spices may be cooked in with the *polo* and meat: onions finely sliced, cloves of garlic, paprika or pinches of turmeric, saffron, cummin seed or coriander; but these are optional.

Enough for four.

KABAB BARG

2 lb. good veal steak	2 medium-sized onions
Juice of 1 lemon	1 egg
3–4 cloves garlic (optional)	Salt to taste

Remove as much fat as possible from the veal. Then cut into small pieces, add the lemon juice, salt, crushed onions and crushed garlic (if used). Mix well together and leave for 2 days in a refrigerator or ice-box. If you haven't one, make the mixture in the morning and cook at night.

When ready for cooking, bind the mixture with an egg, spear it on a *kabab* knife (skewer) and roast over a charcoal fire. As most housewives cook either by gas or electricity, the skewered meat will have to be placed under the grill and turned from time to time as each side cooks.

The meat can be minced instead of cut in pieces: egg and onions will bind the mixture which can then be moulded round the *kabab* knife or skewer.

Enough for six.

CHELO KABAB

This is merely *polo* with two kinds of *kabab*: minced and cut in pieces.

KHORESH (Sauce)

Three kinds of sauce are very popular in Iran: *Bodemjan* (aubergine); *Karafs* (celery); and *Ghorme Sabzy* (vegetables obtainable only in Iran—there is no point, therefore, in discussing this version).

Bodemjan

1 large aubergine	Pinches of paprika, cummin
1 tablespoon butter,	seed, coriander, fenugreek
margarine or oil for frying	and turmeric
1 medium-sized onion	Tomato sauce
3–4 cloves garlic (optional)	

Skin the aubergine and place the vegetable, whole, in a dish. Rub with ½ teaspoon of salt and leave for 2 hours.

Now fry the aubergine in butter or oil till it is dark brown. Crush the onion and add it to the aubergine and butter and fry for a minute or two: then cover with water and boil fast for 15 minutes. The aubergine has by this time disintegrated, so add a couple of tablespoons of tomato sauce and such spices as you wish and cook slowly for 20 minutes.

This should be served with chicken, mutton or beef fried in butter and usually eaten with *polo*.

Karafs is prepared in the same way, substituting celery for aubergine.

43

Fasenjan

Take 1 lb. shelled walnuts, mince finely and fry with 2 chopped onions and 1 dessertspoon of butter. When the oil starts to ooze from the nuts, add 1 wineglass of grenadine juice and 1 dessertspoon of brown sugar. Simmer for 2 hours. Add salt, pepper or/and spices to taste, and serve with meat, chicken or duck.

These recipes were kindly supplied by

MR ESFANDIAR Y BOZORGMEER
THE COQ D'OR RESTAURANT
TEHERAN

PILO

2 breakfast cups fine rice, Kashmiri, Burmese or Patna	3 quarts boiling water
	¼ cup cooking oil

Cover the rice with salt water and soak overnight, then drain.

Place the rice in a thick pan and add 3 quarts of boiling water and cook until almost done. Feel a few grains from time to time between finger and thumb, and if fairly soft but firm, the rice is nearly done.

When this state has been reached, drain off the water and put in the oil. Tilt the pan from side to side till the sides of the pan are coated with oil, then place a thin, clean cloth over the pan and jam on the lid over this.

Now place the pan in a very slow oven—No. 1 if a gas oven, just under 200° if electric; and cook for 3–4 hours.

Pilo may be eaten plain or garnished with chopped onion (raw or fried), garlic and parsley.

It is usually served with *kabab* or some other meat dish.

Enough for 4–6.

CHIRINE PILO (Sweet Rice)

2 breakfast cups rice
1 breakfast cup candied or glazed orange peel, finely diced
¾ cup plump currants

½ breakfast cup blanched slivered almonds (pine kernels may be used instead)
¼ cup cooking oil

Cook the rice as in the recipe for ordinary *pilo*, and when ready, divide it into 3 parts.

Divide the almonds, currants and peel also into 3 parts.

Spread 1 portion of the rice at the bottom of a thick pan, then a portion of the peel, almonds and currants. Then a second layer of rice with peel, almonds and currants, and finally the third layer of rice, with the third layer of peel, almonds and currants.

Then put in the oil, tilt the pan in every direction till the sides of the pan are coated, cover with a thin, clean cloth, and put on the lid. Bake in a slow oven, as before, for 3–4 hours.

Chirine Pilo may be garnished with splintered angelica and crystallized cherries, but if this is done it is eaten on its own, and never with flesh. Otherwise it is usually accompanied by a fried mutton dish.

Enough for 4–6.

IRAQ

SHISH KABAB

('Shish'–Skewer: 'Kabab'—Broiled Meat)

1-lb. leg of very young lamb
½ teaspoon ground cinnamon
½ teaspoon black pepper
6–10 cloves, ground
1 teaspoon ground coriander
1 tablespoon butter, good oil or cooking fat (butter is best)

A good sprinkling of nutmeg
6 tomatoes, sliced
2 onions, sliced
1 breakfast cup Patna, Burma, or other fine rice
Stock or water
Salt to taste
Metal skewers

Soak the rice overnight, then drain. Fry it in the butter till golden brown, then add 1 breakfast cup of stock or water, bring to the boil, then lower heat till the contents just simmer. Now put on a tight-fitting lid and cook till the water has evaporated entirely. The rice should be thoroughly cooked, with each grain separate from the others. If not, add a little more water and cook till this evaporates.

Turn out into a dish and place in a warm—not hot—oven to dry.

Cut the lamb into 1½-inch cubes, but before doing so, mix the ground spices in a little tomato juice so as to make a paste, and rub well into the meat. Put the lamb aside for an hour.

Now put the pieces of lamb on skewers: one piece of lamb, then a slice of onion and finally a slice of tomato; then another piece of lamb, and so on. Grill the skewered lamb over a charcoal fire or under a gas or electric grill till the flesh is tender. Turn the skewers from time to time so that the lamb is cooked on every side.

Serve with the rice and garnish with onions, nuts, sultanas, parsley and/or garlic sliced very finely.

Vary the quantities of ground spices to suit your taste.

The garnish is optional.

Enough for four.

THE SARABIA RESTAURANT
9 OLD BROMPTON ROAD
LONDON, SW7

CHAPTER EIGHT

Dishes of Malaya

THE population of Malaya comprises mainly Malays, Chinese and Indians, the majority from South India and Ceylon, with a sprinkling of Sikhs and Pathans; and a small but influential Arab community, most of whom come from Hadramaut, in Arabia.

As a result there is a similarity between Indian and Malayan food, though Malayan curries have a distinct tang, appearance and even aroma of their own, and no one with a discriminating palate would mistake a Malayan curry for an Indian curry.

BANANA CURRY

4 large, unripe bananas
1 tablespoon small onions, sliced
1 green chilli, sliced
1 tablespoon pounded Bombay duck
¼ teaspoon fenugreek
2 breakfast cups coconut milk, which can be extracted from ½ lb. desiccated coconut

A pinch (⅛ teaspoon) of ground saffron or turmeric
1-inch stick of cinnamon
1-inch piece of *rampe*
3–4 curry leaves
1 sprig fennel
2 tablespoons coconut oil, ghee, butter, mustard oil or margarine
1 teaspoon salt

Skin the bananas; slit them lengthwise and then in half; rub them with the salt and saffron or turmeric and fry them in oil.

Now pour the coconut milk into a saucepan with the other ingredients, bring to the boil and simmer for 30 minutes. Then add the bananas and simmer till the gravy is thick.

Use bananas with the skin as green as possible, and use 2–3 chillies if you like it more pungent.

Enough for two.

FRIED EGG CURRY

This is a popular curry and far more spicy than egg curries concocted in India, Turkey and elsewhere.

8 large eggs
1 tablespoon onion, finely sliced
4 cloves garlic, chopped
1-inch slice of green ginger, chopped
1 small piece of *rampe*
$\frac{1}{2}$ stem lemon grass
3–4 curry leaves
2-inch stick of cinnamon
1 sprig fennel
3 teaspoons coriander seed
$1\frac{1}{2}$ teaspoons white cummin seed

$\frac{1}{4}$ teaspoon sweet cummin seed
$\frac{1}{2}$ teaspoon fenugreek
Juice of 1 lemon
$\frac{1}{2}$ lb. desiccated coconut—to make 2 breakfast cups coconut milk
2 dessertspoons Bombay duck, broken up
5 red chillies, ground
$\frac{1}{2}$ teaspoon turmeric
A pinch of salt
1 tablespoon frying fat, butter or oil

Boil eggs very hard, then shell and rub with the salt and turmeric, and fry to a light-brown colour. It is advisable to prick the eggs all over with a hat-pin or similar instrument, otherwise they are likely to explode when fried.

Now fry half the onion in a dessertspoon of fat, together with the *rampe*, lemon grass and curry leaves; then pour in the coconut milk and remainder of the ingredients—except the lemon juice.

Simmer till the gravy is thick, stirring the while; then add the eggs, cover with the gravy, spooning it over the eggs again and again, then put in the lemon juice. Simmer for 10 minutes, then serve.

Enough for four.

YELLOW RICE

2 breakfast cups table rice
(Patna, Burma or Kashmiri)

¼ lb. ghee, butter, dripping or
best margarine

½ lb. onions, finely sliced

¼ lb. Bombay duck, pounded

10 cloves

20–30 peppercorns

10 cardamoms, ground or
powdered to bring out
flavour

1 sprig fennel

2-inch piece of *rampe*

½ stem lemon grass

3–4 curry leaves

1 *full* teaspoon ground
turmeric for colouring (or
saffron)

Milk of 2 coconuts, or milk
from 1 lb. desiccated
coconut—2 breakfast cups

Salt to taste

Heat the fat and fry in it about a third of the onions, *rampe* and
lemon grass and the curry leaves.

When the onions are well browned, mix in the rice, cook briskly
for about 5 minutes, stirring all the time; then add the coconut milk
and the remainder of the ingredients except the cardamoms, which
must be added when the rice is half cooked. Some prefer not to
grind or powder the cardamoms, but to mix the seeds into the rice
after it has been cooked.

If coconut milk is not available or you would rather not use milk
made from desiccated coconut, the rice may be boiled either in meat
or vegetable stock, or a mixture of both.

The rice is thoroughly cooked when each grain is separate from
the others and yet soft enough to be eaten. If there is any stock or
coconut milk left when this state is reached, drain it off; if there is
not enough liquid, add a little boiling water.

Yellow rice is served with curry.

Enough for 4–5.

CHICKEN GRAVY CURRY WITH PULWAL

1 chicken
2 oz. ghee, mustard oil,
  coconut oil or other
  cooking fat
1½ teaspoons salt
4 teaspoons ground onions
1 teaspoon ground turmeric
1 teaspoon ground chilli
½ teaspoon ground ginger
2 blades lemon grass

¼ teaspoon ground garlic
2 large cups coconut milk
  (the milk from 1 large
  coconut)
3–4 cloves—ground or whole
3–4 cardamoms—ground or
  whole
3–4 1-inch sticks of
  cinnamon, ground

Take a plump chicken, bone it and mince the flesh as finely as possible, till it is reduced to a pulp. Mix the flesh and salt with the spices given, using onion, turmeric, chilli, ginger, garlic, cloves, cardamom and cinnamon, but first fry these spices in heated ghee or fat or oil, in a thick saucepan.

Then take a dozen or more large *pulwals* (the *pulwal* is a vegetable like a large squat pea, but much greater in diameter), slit them down one side, and scrape away the seeds from inside. Wash the *pulwals*, and stuff them with the forcemeat. This done, join the sides together and tie with cotton and cook in coconut milk (2 breakfast cups), adding a couple of blades of lemon grass to the liquid; these must be removed before serving. Bring to the boil; simmer for 30–40 minutes. Serve with rice.

Enough for four.

Pulwals may be had in cans from any store that sells Indian curry spices, and, like okras (Lady's Fingers), have a flavour quite distinct from vegetables grown in Europe.

Either prawns or fish may be treated in much the same way and stuffed into *pulwal*, and both are favourite dishes.

LIVER CURRY

2 lb. liver
10–20 red chillies, ground
2 dessertspoons white cummin seed, ground
1½ tablespoons small onions, sliced
8 cloves garlic, either whole or chopped
3 1-inch slices of green ginger, chopped
3 1-inch pieces of *rampe*
½ stem lemon grass
1 sprig curry leaves
Salt to taste

3 pieces of aromatic ginger, powdered
20 cardamoms, either whole or powdered
1 teaspoon fenugreek
1 wineglass (sherry size) best wine vinegar
1 tablespoon ghee, dripping, mustard oil or margarine
2 breakfast cups coconut milk; if this is made from desiccated coconut, use about 1 lb.

Boil the liver till firm, then cut it lengthwise into strips, and chop the strips into pieces about 1 inch long.

Place the liver, coconut milk and all the ingredients, except the fat, into a saucepan with a thick bottom and boil till the liver is soft.

Now drain off the liquid, put in the fat and fry liver and ingredients till well browned; then pour back the liquid and simmer, stirring the while, till the gravy thickens. To be eaten with rice.

Enough for six.

FISH PUDICHCHI

2 large slices of cod or other coarse fish, each about 1 lb.
10 red chillies, pounded (or less)
1 teaspoon ground turmeric
1 tablespoon onion, finely sliced
4–6 cloves garlic, chopped or whole
3-inch stick of cinnamon

3 1-inch slices of green ginger, chopped
1-inch piece of *rampe*
½ stem lemon grass
1 sprig curry leaves
½ teaspoon fenugreek
2 breakfast cups coconut milk
Juice of 1 lemon
Salt to taste

51

Quarter each slice of fish and place in a thick saucepan. Add all the ingredients except the lemon juice, and boil. When the fish is soft but not cooked through, add the lemon juice; then finish cooking.

This is one of the few Eastern dishes in which fat is not used.

Enough for four.

PRAWN CURRY

½ lb. dried prawns (if fresh, use double the quantity)
10 large half-ripe tomatoes, sliced
10 dried chillies, pounded (as many as 40 are used in Malaya)
2 tablespoons pounded Bombay duck
1 large onion, sliced finely
1 teaspoon ground turmeric
2-inch piece of green ginger, chopped
1-inch piece of *rampe*
¼ stem lemon grass
4–5 curry leaves
3 breakfast cups coconut milk
Juice from 1 oz. tamarind in hot water
1 tablespoon ghee, butter, margarine, or coconut oil
6 cloves garlic, chopped

Fry the *rampe*, lemon grass, curry leaves and onion in the fat. Mix the remainder of the ingredients together, and when the onion is golden brown, pour them in, and bring to the boil. When the prawns are nearly soft, turn down the heat and simmer till the gravy has almost all evaporated.

Eaten usually with yellow rice or *pilau*.

Enough for four.

These recipes were kindly supplied by

MR K. THARMARATNAM
SECOND SECRETARY, MALAYA HOUSE
57 TRAFALGAR SQUARE
LONDON, WC2

FISH CURRY

1 large teacup cooked fish
1 small cooking apple
½ onion
1 tablespoon butter
1 small teacup milk and water in equal amounts
1 teaspoon flour
1 tablespoon grated coconut
3 tablespoons rice
A squeeze of lemon
Salt and pepper to taste
1 teaspoon curry powder

Peel and chop both the apple and onion. Melt the butter in a saucepan, add the apple and onion and fry till golden brown. Then stir in the curry powder and flour, pour in the milk and water and bring to the boil. Simmer for 30 minutes (this is the curry sauce).

Prepare the cooked fish in large flakes.

Boil the rice till soft, drain off water, and dry.

Now add the fish to the curry sauce and sprinkle in cayenne and salt, and squeeze in the lemon juice. If, after making this dish once, you find there is too little lemon, add more next time. Heat fish and curry sauce but do NOT boil.

To dish: make a border of the boiled rice, pour the curried fish into the middle and sprinkle with either white or browned coconut. Garnish with 'butterflies' of lemon, and/or parsley, and chilli skins. Serve with sweet mango chutney.

Enough for two.

In Malaya this dish is served to the accompaniment of sliced banana (uncooked), sliced banana fried brown, pineapple diced small, salted ground-nuts (peanuts), grated coconut either raw or browned, ground red peppers, *brinjals*, okras and sultanas.

You can vary this curry by using ½ lb. fresh prawns, cooked beef, chicken or game instead of fish. It is an easy curry to prepare and specially suitable for beginners.

MRS G. K. RAMESHWAR
17-D LIM TUA TOW ROAD
SINGAPORE, 19
MALAYA

CHAPTER NINE

Dishes of Turkey

CURRIES proper—that is, curries rich in chilli, cummin, coriander, cardamom, cinnamon, fenugreek, turmeric and saffron—emanated doubtless from India (including what is now Pakistan), Ceylon, Burma, Malaya and Indonesia; but for 4000 years or more rice has been eaten as far west as Egypt and as far east as China, Japan and the Philippines.

As rice goes hand in hand with savoury foods, it is little wonder that Turkey, too, that land of Empire-builders, is the country where the *pilav* (*pilaf* or *pilao*) was born.

The Turks are noted gourmets. In Istanbul, Turkey's mysterious metropolis, men choose their drinking water as Parisians choose their wines, and a mere sip serves to identify the spring from whence it gushes.

This sensitivity to nuances reflects the Turk's aesthetic approach to life. He is easily the 'choosiest' eater in all Europe, with an Oriental rather than an Occidental outlook on food. The discriminating Turk never asks for an 'apple', but for an *Amasya* or a *Gumashane*; and if for a pear, when it was plucked from the tree!

His cuisine is the best balanced (from a dietetic point of view) in Europe, and the variety of his sauces, creams and blends of food would turn most Parisians electric green with envy. The aubergine, alone, is cooked in more than forty different ways.

In a volume as slim as this it is possible to give only a handful of Turkish recipes; and those the simplest and most easily concocted.

Turkey, once the cross-roads of the civilized world, has borrowed from both East and West and has contrived both kinds of cuisine into a blend that is distinctly her own.

If you dine with a Turk in his country he will start the meal with the salutation, 'May it give you good health,' adding the words, 'and happy eating, too'. Only thus can food benefit you to the utmost.

TURQUOISE (Yogurt Soup)

3 medium-sized cucumbers
¼ teaspoon salt
1–2 cloves garlic
1 tablespoon best malt vinegar
1 teaspoon dill
1 pint yogurt (4 bottles)

1 onion (optional)
2 tablespoons olive oil
1 tablespoon chopped mint
  or ½ teaspoon dried mint
  leaves

Peel the cucumbers (some prefer them unpeeled), quarter lengthwise, and slice about ⅛ inch thick. Place in a bowl and sprinkle with salt.

Rub another bowl with the garlic and swish the vinegar around it to collect the flavour (discarding the garlic); or, preferably, slice or mash the garlic into the vinegar. The onion, if used, may be put in, finely chopped, at this stage. Next add the dill and yogurt and stir till the mixture has the consistency of thick soup. If too thick, add cold water. Pour over the cucumbers and stir.

Serve cold, sprinkled with the olive oil and garnished with the chopped mint. In winter the soup may be served hot, and for those who cannot stomach it, the olive oil may be omitted. In summer, chill before serving.

Enough for four.

DOLMAS

Dolmas are a feature of Turkish food; *dolma* comes from *doldurmak* —to stuff.

1 lb. ground lamb or beef free
  from fat
1 large chopped onion

1 teaspoon chopped dill
½ teaspoon cummin seed
  (optional)

55

3–4 cloves garlic, crushed	Salt and pepper
$\frac{1}{4}$ cup rice	A pinch of chilli powder
1 teaspoon chopped mint	(optional)
1 teaspoon ground coriander seed (optional)	1 tablespoon tomato sauce (optional)

These ingredients comprise the stuffing. Vary them, at times using the optional spices, at times leaving them out till you find which you like best.

Place the meat in a bowl and add the onion, garlic, rice, mint, dill, the remainder of the spices, and the tomato sauce, if you are going to use these. Knead well.

If aubergines are to be stuffed, choose short, fat, round specimens that will cook upright in a pan. Cut off the stem end and keep it for a cover. Peel the aubergine lengthwise, in strips, leaving alternate unpeeled layers to strengthen the aubergine. Scoop out the inside leaving a shell less than 1 inch thick. Fill with the stuffing and replace the stem-end cover.

Don't waste the inside of the aubergine, which has been scooped out; this, cooked with onion, garlic, tomato and a little lemon juice, forms an excellent addition to any dish such as *kabab*.

If green peppers are to be stuffed, slit through the tops but don't sever them. Then remove the seeds and membranes, fill with stuffing and close.

Tomato *dolmas* can be prepared in the same way as green pepper *dolmas*.

Zucchini Dolmas (Squash)

Clean the outside of the squash (or marrow), cut off the narrow end and use this as a cover. Scoop out the inside, leaving a $\frac{1}{2}$-inch shell, then stuff and replace the cover, fastening it with toothpicks or cocktail sticks.

Sometimes one prepares all the *dolmas* together. When this is done place the aubergine and *zucchini dolmas* on the bottom of a la ge saucepan; on top, a layer of green pepper *dolmas*, and over them a layer of tomato *dolmas*.

Then put in 2 tablespoons of butter and a breakfast cup of water, put on a well-fitting cover and cook on a medium heat for 30–40 minutes, or until the vegetables are soft.

If any stuffing is left over, make it into meat balls and place between the stuffed *dolmas* in the saucepan.

All these *dolmas* may be cooked separately or together, but the quantities given for stuffing ingredients are enough only for four persons.

ROAST CHICKEN WITH PINE-NUT STUFFING

1 roasting chicken	3–4 cardamoms, shelled
1 breakfast cup rice	(optional)
¼ breakfast cup currants	A pinch each of ground
¼ breakfast cup *pignolia* (pine	coriander seed and chilli
kernels)	powder (optional)
3 tablespoons butter	3–4 cloves garlic (optional)
¼ teaspoon ground ginger	2 cups water
(optional)	Salt to taste

Prepare the chicken for roasting. Cover the rice with lukewarm water and allow it to stand. Take out the chicken liver and chop it into small pieces.

Clean the currants and nuts, then melt 1 tablespoon of butter in a large saucepan and *sauté* (fry quickly and lightly) the nuts until they turn pink.

Remove the nuts and *sauté* the chicken liver in the same butter. Now return the nuts to the pan (with liver) and add the currants, rice (washed and drained), salt (and ginger, cardamoms, garlic, coriander and chilli, if used) and 2 cups of boiling water.

Cover and stew slowly over a medium heat. When the water is absorbed, add 2 tablespoons of butter and mix well. Then remove from the stove and place in a warm oven (uncovered) for 15 minutes.

The rice should by this time be fluffy with every grain separate.

Fill the chicken loosely with this stuffing till it is about two-thirds full and sew or skewer the opening. Then roast as usual.

There is no hard and fast rule for this dish; experiment with the spices and leave out those you do not like—if any. Walnuts or chestnuts may be used instead of pine kernels.

Enough for six.

57

KORISTCH

2-lb. shoulder of mutton	½ lb. stewed prunes—half
1 teaspoon pepper	stewed and still firm
½ teaspoon salt	5 1-inch sticks of cinnamon
8 finely sliced onions	4 tablespoons ghee,
4–6 cloves	margarine or butter

Bone the mutton, rub thoroughly with the salt and pepper, roll and tie with string.

Heat the fat in a thick saucepan and fry the onions till brown. Then put in the mutton and well brown all over.

Now add just enough water to prevent the onions from scorching, put in the cinnamon and cloves, cover the pan and simmer till the meat is tender and the liquid absorbed. If the meat is not tender and the liquid has evaporated, add a little more water or stock.

Then put in the half-stewed prunes and baste the meat with the prune syrup. Turn down the heat till the contents of the pan just simmer gently and keep on till the prunes are soft and mushy.

Sultanas may be added with the prunes, or half prunes and half sultanas; and 3–4 cloves of garlic may also be put in after the meat is tender, and before the prunes are added. Some like garlic and think that it improves the flavour; others think that the dish is much too strong with garlic and omit it.

Enough for six.

SHISH KABAB

2-lb. leg of lamb	2–3 bay leaves—or more
1 tablespoon olive oil	Green pepper (optional)
Juice of 1 lemon	Aubergine (optional)
1 medium-sized onion, thickly sliced	Salt and pepper to taste
3 medium-sized tomatoes, sliced	Pinches of other spices (optional)—cummin, chilli, coriander
3–4 cloves garlic (optional)	Metal skewers or spits

Cut the meat into 1-inch cubes. Mix the olive oil and lemon juice, and if garlic is used, mash this in. Rub this mixture into the meat. Place it in a dish, sprinkle with salt and pepper (and if other spices are used, with them, too), and put away for 6 hours.

Then take the spits or skewers, and spear on them in turn a piece of meat, slice of tomato, slice of onion, piece of bay leaf; and so on; meat, tomato, onion, bay leaf . . . .

If green peppers or aubergines are used, insert a piece of pepper or aubergine, or both, on to the skewers at intervals.

Grill slowly over a charcoal or wood fire, or an open coal fire. Where these are not available, an electric or gas grill will do. Turn the spits as you grill.

Enough for four.

LADY MEAT BALLS

1 lb. finely ground lean mutton
3 large onions (diced)
½ cup rice
½ cup grated cheese
1 teaspoon chopped parsley
1 teaspoon chopped dill
⅛ teaspoon pepper

⅛ teaspoon chilli powder
½ cup flour
4 eggs
2–3 cloves garlic
¼ cup shortening or lard
Salt to taste

Put the mutton (or lamb, if you like), onions and garlic through the grinder. Boil the rice till tender, drain away water, and mix with the onions and garlic, then with the cheese, parsley, dill, pepper, chilli powder and salt. Knead well for 5 minutes, form into egg-sized ovals and roll in flour. Beat the eggs till frothy, then dip the meat ovals into the egg and fry all over in the shortening.

Enough, with vegetables, for four.

LENTIL MEAT STEW

1 cup red lentils
1 large onion, chopped
4 cloves garlic, whole
1 tablespoon butter
1 lb. beef or lamb cut into
    1-inch cubes
1 teaspoon salt
¼ teaspoon pepper

⅛ teaspoon chilli powder
1 teaspoon turmeric
½ teaspoon cummin, ground
¼ cup rice
2 cups water
Vinegar to taste (optional)
Juice of 1 lemon (optional)

59

Wash the lentils, put into a thick saucepan and cover with water. Soak overnight and then drain. Brown the chopped onion and garlic in butter and add lentils; then the meat and enough water to cover (about a cupful), and salt, pepper, chilli, cummin and turmeric. Bring to the boil, then simmer gently (about an hour), add the rice and another cup of water. Simmer, stir well, then cook for 20–30 minutes till rice is cooked through. If you wish, add vinegar or lemon juice before serving.

Enough for four.

PILAV

2 breakfast cups rice	2 teaspoons salt—or less—to
4 medium-sized tomatoes	taste
(fresh or canned)	3½ breakfast cups vegetable
2 oz. butter	or meat stock, or chicken
3 cloves garlic (optional)	broth

Wash the rice well, and drain, then set aside. Peel the tomatoes, then cut them into small chunks and seed them, though this is not essential.

Heat butter and tomatoes together till a tomato paste is obtained. If garlic is used, cook it with the butter and tomatoes. Add the stock and salt to this mixture and boil for 2 minutes.

While still boiling, pour in the rice, stir once, cover and simmer without stirring till the rice has absorbed all the liquid. Now turn the flame very low and simmer for another 20 minutes.

Remove from the stove and leave uncovered for 30 minutes—but do not stir.

When transferring rice to the serving dish, use a flat serving spoon and handle the rice gently to keep it fluffy.

Enough for six.

Coffee is a beverage drunk in few Eastern countries outside the Arab zone, and generally speaking the making of good coffee is not understood in India, Ceylon, Burma, Malaya and Indonesia.

The Turks, however, are connoisseurs of coffee, and black coffee made in the Turkish way is well worth sampling.

TURKISH COFFEE

    2 tablespoons brown sugar   2 teaspoons pulverized coffee
       (Demerara or Barbadoes)   ½ breakfast cup water

Turkish coffee is made in a *jezve*—a cylindrical pot with a long handle, sold in shops specializing in Mediterranean food. In London, a *jezve* may be bought in Soho.*

Turkish coffee is roasted to a darker brown than coffee from the West Indies, Kenya, India or South America, and is far more bitter to the palate. It should be taken after breakfast or lunch when, according to Dr Bernard Aschner, it restores a flabby or hyper-acid stomach with no harm to the heart. It keeps you awake and enables you to conduct business, with all your faculties alert, even after a heavy lunch. It should NOT be taken at night.

Put cold water in the *jezve*. Add sugar and coffee. Stir well.

Place the *jezve* over a low flame and cook till the coffee and water rise to the boil. The surface will be covered by froth. Pour this off into two *demi-tasse* cups. Then bring the liquid to the boil again and remove from the fire, or stove. Pour the coffee over the froth to fill the cups, and serve.

Vary the proportions of coffee and sugar to suit your taste; but remember, Turkish coffee is NEVER taken with either milk or cream. It always has a froth on it. You can add milk or cream, but it won't be *Turkish* coffee.

Enough for two.

* Obtainable from Madame Cadec of 27 Greek Street, London, W1.

Addresses of Curry-spice Suppliers

CURRY SPICES MAY BE OBTAINED BY POST FROM:

Jamshid's Spice Box,
19 Old Brompton Road,
London, SW7

Harrod's (Food Dept),
Knightsbridge,
London, SW1

Lal Jolly,
70 Warwick Road,
Earls Court, London, SW5

Selfridge's (Food Stores),
Oxford Street,
London, W1

The Bombay Emporium,
70 Grafton Way,
London, W1

Express Dairy Co.,
212 Earl's Court Road,
London, SW5

A. Abdullah & Son,
2 Helmet Street,
London, EC2

Percy C. Richardson & Sons,
33a Brigstock Road,
Thornton Heath, Surrey

R. Dell & Sons,
127 King Street,
Hammersmith, London, W6

R. Brooks & Co.,
27 Maiden Lane,
London, WC2

also at
33 Tachbrook Street,
London, SW1

M. O. & E. A. Dell,
431 North End Road,
London, SW6

John Little & Son,
Eastgate Row,
Chester

Army & Navy Stores,
Victoria Street,
London, SW1

William Jones Ltd.,
48/50 Bridge Street,
Chester

Cottle Brothers,
20/22 Queen Victoria Street,
Reading

L. Palm Ltd.
The Market,
Oxford

Grimbly Hughes,
Corn Market Street,
Oxford

Index

A

Ajam Panggang, 37

B

Balachaung, 15
Banana Curry, 47
Beef Curry, 26
Bodemjan, 43
Brinjal Pohie, 19

C

Chelo Kabab, 43
Chicken Curry, 22
Chicken Gravy Curry
  with Pulwal, 50
Chicken Kaukswe, 16
Chicken Korma, 34
Chirine Pilo, 45
Coconut Rice, 18
Crab Curry, 30

D

Dolmas, 55
Dove or Wood pigeon, 40
Duck Curry, 18

E

Egg Stew, 21

F

Fasenjan, 44
Fish Curry, 14, 29, 52
Fish Pudichchi, 51
Fried Egg Curry, 48
Fried Potatoes, 22

H

Hot Stew with Rice, 23

K

Kabab Barg, 42
Karafs, 43
Khoresh, 43
Koritsch, 58

L

Lady Meat Balls, 59
Lentil Meat Stew, 59
Liver Curry, 51

M

Mologothannie, 24
Moong Dhall, 33

N

Nasi Kuning, 38
Nga-Daung-Doke, 12

O

Otak-Otak, 37
Ox-Heart Black Curry, 27

P

Pilav, 60
Polo, 41
Prawn Currey, 52
Prawn and Tomato Curry, 16

R

Rama's Bath, 39
Roast Chicken with Pine-nut
  Stuffing, 57
Roast Duck, 17

S

Sate Ajam, 36
Sathé Curry, 25

Serikaya, 39
Serpathala 31
Shami Kabab or Cabob, 33
Sha-Nga-Boung, 13
Shish Kabab, 45, 58
Smoked Fish, 14
Soto Ajam, 35
Spicy Ceylonese Pork Curry, 28
Steamed Fish, 14
Stuffed Chilli Curry, 20

T

Tahchin Bareh, 42
Tahchin Esfenádj, 42

Turkish Coffee, 61
Turquoise, 55

V

Vegetable Pilau, 32
Very Young Milk Shark Curry, 28

Y

Yellow Rice, 49

Z

Zucchini Dolmas, 56